TELEVISION

What's Behind What You See

From the latin word _ridere_, meaning "to see"

Shortened, it becomes "TV"

VISION
What's Behind What You See

W. Carter Merbreier

Known to generations of Philadelphia-area children
as the host of WPVI-TV's *Captain Noah and His Magical Ark*

WITH LINDA CAPUS RILEY

Pictures by Michael Chesworth

Captain Noah

Farrar, Straus and Giroux   New York

Television Sends Pictures Through the Air

Television is astonishing. It alters our daily lives. It affects how we think. All because of its incredible ability to change what a camera views into an electrical signal that can be sent through the air to a TV set, bringing into our homes the sights and sounds of distant countries, and the best and worst of other people's ideas and adventures. Television is a modern technological marvel.

Every broadcast TV station has its own name, made up of three or four call letters. Most stations west of the Mississippi River begin their call letters with a "K." Stations east of the Mississippi usually begin with a "W."

A TV camera picks up light from a scene and stores the light energy for an instant while translating it into an electrical video signal. Sixty times a second, the camera sends out an electrical picture of what it "sees."

The indicator light turns on to tell the performer when the camera is transmitting a picture.

The viewfinder is a miniature TV screen that shows the operator exactly what the camera is viewing.

A studio camera rests on a sturdy wheeled platform called a dolly.

A microphone changes sound into an electrical audio signal.

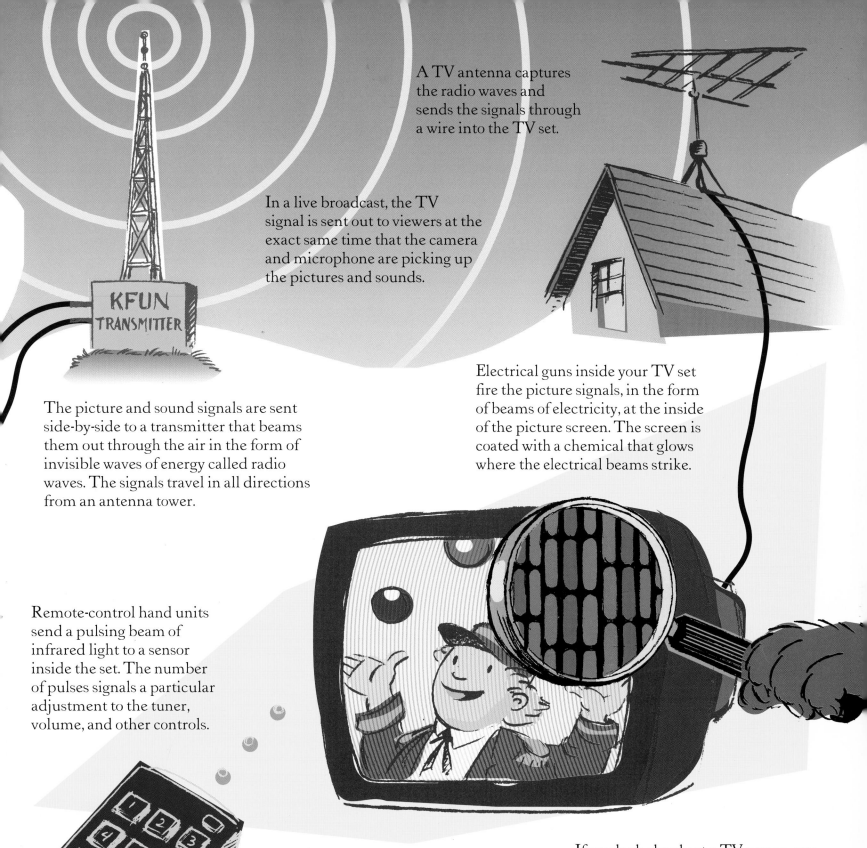

A TV antenna captures the radio waves and sends the signals through a wire into the TV set.

In a live broadcast, the TV signal is sent out to viewers at the exact same time that the camera and microphone are picking up the pictures and sounds.

The picture and sound signals are sent side-by-side to a transmitter that beams them out through the air in the form of invisible waves of energy called radio waves. The signals travel in all directions from an antenna tower.

KFUN TRANSMITTER

Electrical guns inside your TV set fire the picture signals, in the form of beams of electricity, at the inside of the picture screen. The screen is coated with a chemical that glows where the electrical beams strike.

Remote-control hand units send a pulsing beam of infrared light to a sensor inside the set. The number of pulses signals a particular adjustment to the tuner, volume, and other controls.

A TV signal travels a kind of invisible highway called a channel. Each channel has room for only one station's signal. When you dial a station's assigned channel number, you are directing your set to receive only signals from that station.

If you look closely at a TV screen, you will see many tiny lines or, on older sets, dots. The beams scan back and forth across the entire screen, sixty times per second, striking these lines or dots to reproduce exactly the same pattern of light picked up by the camera.

Inside a Local TV Station

News, sports, children's programs, and talk shows are often created at a local broadcast station. Working at a TV station is like being part of a team that puts together a giant jigsaw puzzle every day. The TV programs must fit together perfectly, and be ready to send out to the audience at exactly the right time.

Ten times more video is shot for a news story than appears on the air. Rarely is it shot in the order in which it is to be broadcast. A video editor must shorten and rearrange the raw footage.

Artists create maps and other graphics, such as sports team logos or charts showing election results, for the news show.

ART ROOM

EDITING BOOTH

Half the people at the station work here. It's the busiest place in the building.

NEWSROOM

Businesses buy ad time on TV to tell the audience about their products. The TV station uses the money to create or buy programs.

SALES OFFICE

RECEPTION

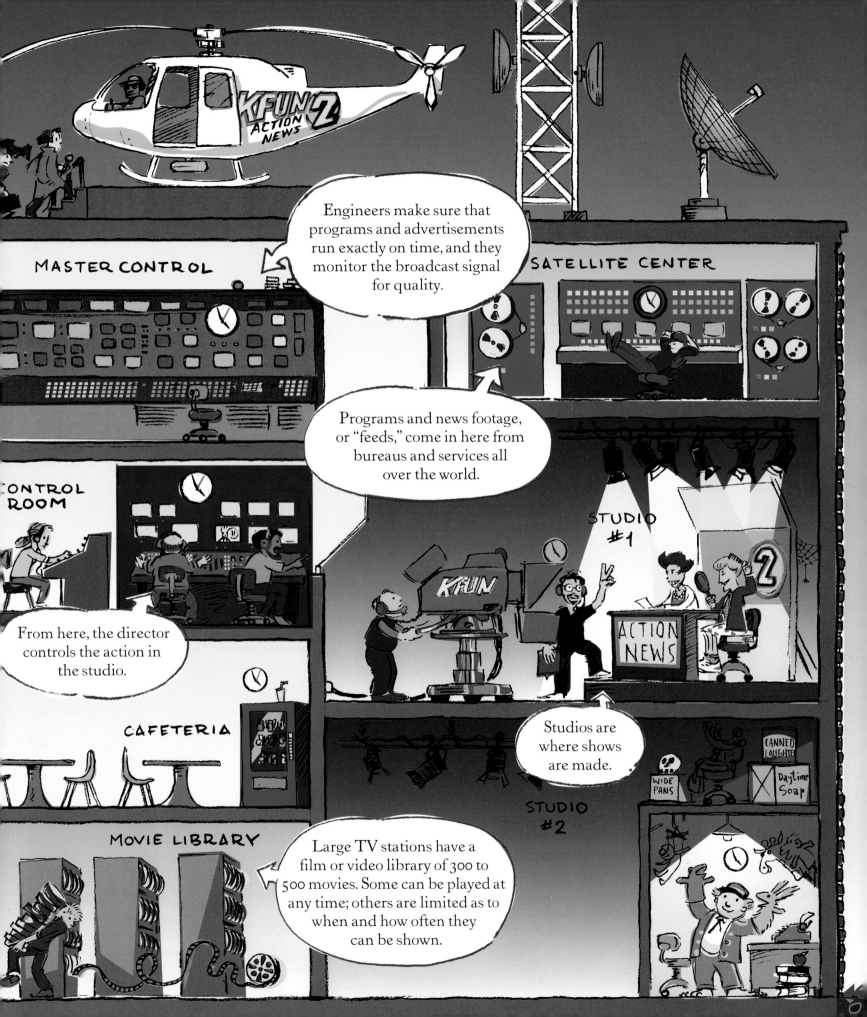

"Birds" Bounce Signals Around the World

TV signals sent through the air travel in straight lines. They cannot curve with the shape of the earth. As the earth curves, these signals keep going—into outer space. TV satellites are unmanned space vehicles orbiting about 23,000 miles above the earth that are used to send signals around the planet. Before the Telstar I satellite was launched into space in 1962, there was no way to see a live broadcast of an event on the other side of the world. But now it's commonplace.

The satellite receives the uplink, strengthens it, and then transmits a downlink that can be picked up by other Earth stations.

In a satellite broadcast, a station on Earth transmits a TV signal to a satellite known as an uplink.

Panels of solar cells on the satellite's outer surface power its batteries, using the sun's light.

USE NO HOOKS

RENT THIS SPACE

UPLINK

The signal travels the 46,000 miles up and down in less than a second.

A satellite carries a ten-year supply of fuel for the miniature jets that keep it at its fixed position above the planet. If a satellite starts to drift, the jets are fired by controllers on Earth to bring it back into place.

No one knows I exist.

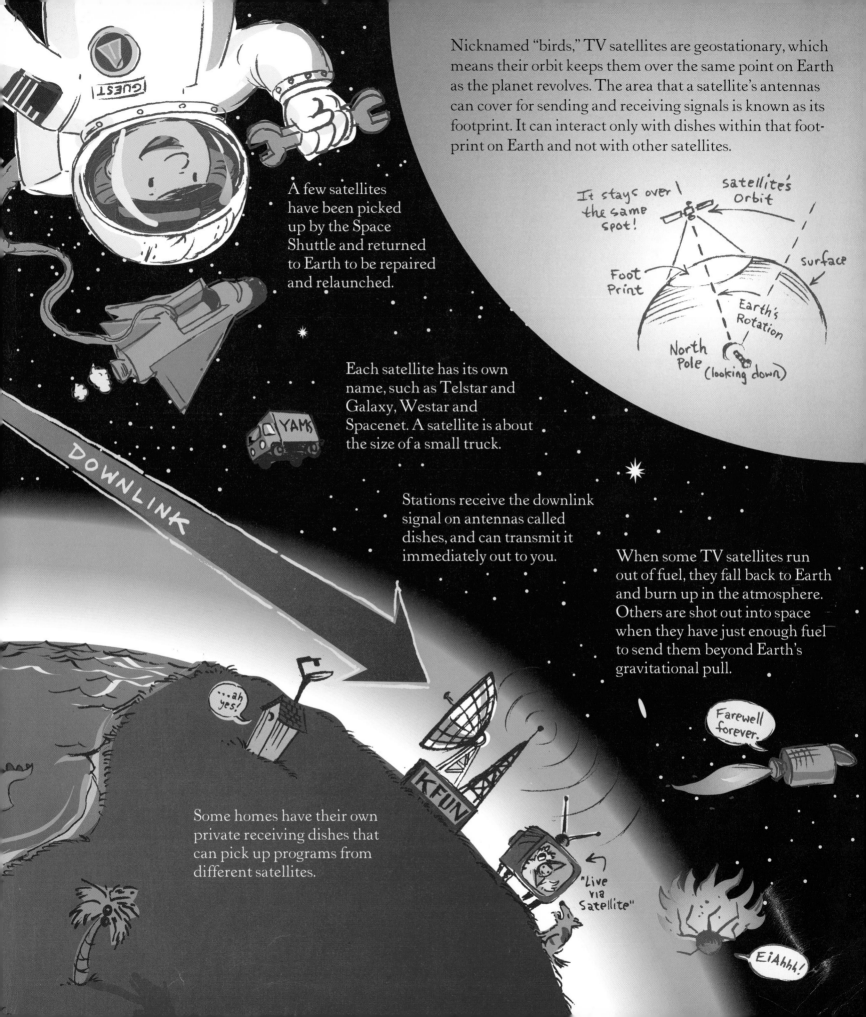

Nicknamed "birds," TV satellites are geostationary, which means their orbit keeps them over the same point on Earth as the planet revolves. The area that a satellite's antennas can cover for sending and receiving signals is known as its footprint. It can interact only with dishes within that footprint on Earth and not with other satellites.

A few satellites have been picked up by the Space Shuttle and returned to Earth to be repaired and relaunched.

Each satellite has its own name, such as Telstar and Galaxy, Westar and Spacenet. A satellite is about the size of a small truck.

Stations receive the downlink signal on antennas called dishes, and can transmit it immediately out to you.

When some TV satellites run out of fuel, they fall back to Earth and burn up in the atmosphere. Others are shot out into space when they have just enough fuel to send them beyond Earth's gravitational pull.

Some homes have their own private receiving dishes that can pick up programs from different satellites.

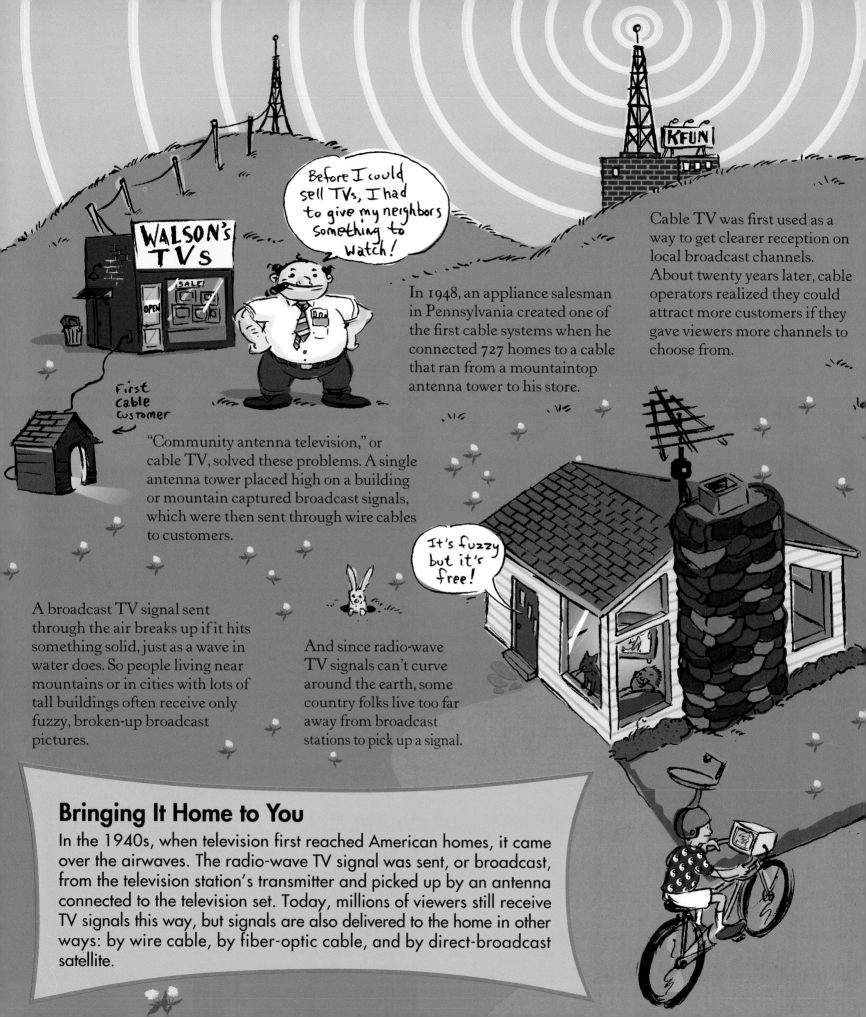

Before I could sell TVs, I had to give my neighbors something to watch!

In 1948, an appliance salesman in Pennsylvania created one of the first cable systems when he connected 727 homes to a cable that ran from a mountaintop antenna tower to his store.

Cable TV was first used as a way to get clearer reception on local broadcast channels. About twenty years later, cable operators realized they could attract more customers if they gave viewers more channels to choose from.

WALSON'S TVs

SALE!

OPEN

First cable customer

"Community antenna television," or cable TV, solved these problems. A single antenna tower placed high on a building or mountain captured broadcast signals, which were then sent through wire cables to customers.

It's fuzzy but it's free!

A broadcast TV signal sent through the air breaks up if it hits something solid, just as a wave in water does. So people living near mountains or in cities with lots of tall buildings often receive only fuzzy, broken-up broadcast pictures.

And since radio-wave TV signals can't curve around the earth, some country folks live too far away from broadcast stations to pick up a signal.

Bringing It Home to You

In the 1940s, when television first reached American homes, it came over the airwaves. The radio-wave TV signal was sent, or broadcast, from the television station's transmitter and picked up by an antenna connected to the television set. Today, millions of viewers still receive TV signals this way, but signals are also delivered to the home in other ways: by wire cable, by fiber-optic cable, and by direct-broadcast satellite.

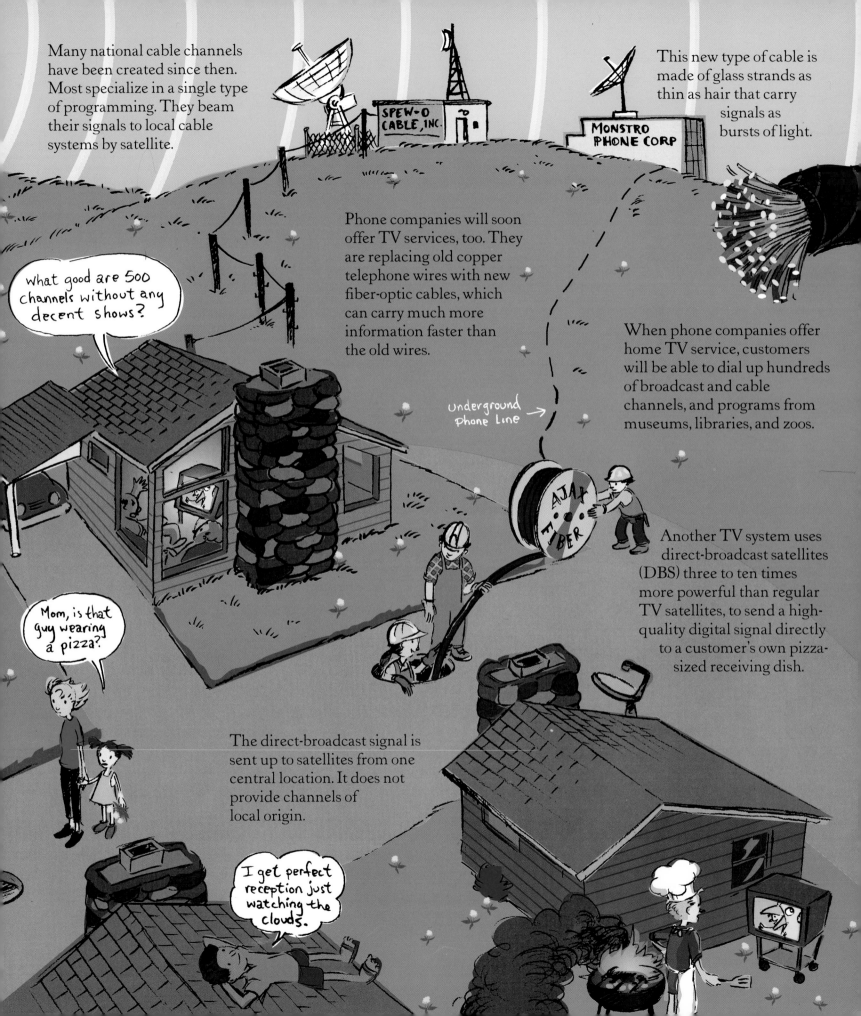

How Programmers Plan the Day

There are more than 92 million households in the United States with at least one TV, and a total of 235 million viewers. TV programmers specialize in predicting what style of program will attract the largest number of viewers at a particular time during the broadcast day. This requires studying reports on the age, sex, and interests of an audience, a knowledge of all the programs in production, and a gut feeling about what people will want to watch.

TRUCKERS WHO LOVE CATS

Late morning and late afternoon have become talk-show territory. Talk shows are inexpensive to produce because there's just one set, one host, few if any writers, and the guests appear free or are paid very little.

Early-morning programming is split between cartoons and wake-up news-magazine shows. This is the time when families are getting ready for school and for work, and different TV stations offer them choices: for parents to catch up on the news, or for kids to be entertained while Mom and Dad shower and dress.

The networks devote afternoons to daily melodramas better known as soap operas because the advertisers are often detergent manufacturers trying to reach homemakers. Soap operas are more expensive to produce than talk shows: they require several sets, many actors, and scripts for five days a week. But they draw a loyal audience.

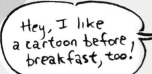

Hey, I like a cartoon before breakfast, too!

RERUNS
After a show has been on the air for a few seasons, its producers will have enough old episodes to sell or rent for repeat showings, called reruns.

It's channel surfing time!

Late afternoons are split between talk shows and shows for the after-school crowd. There are lots of reruns of old comedies plus cartoons and a few kid-oriented variety programs.

Prime time is the later part of the evening, when the whole family is available to watch TV and all the stations are battling for their share of this large audience. The goal is to get the biggest audience possible to tune in early in the evening, and to keep that audience until bedtime.

Early evening on the networks and their affiliates is devoted to news. Other stations try to offer appealing alternative programs, such as reruns of popular old shows. The hour following the news is a programming grab bag, with some stations airing game shows, and others scheduling reruns, entertainment news, or true-to-life police, fire, and rescue shows.

Where's dinner, guys....?

NETWORKS

Most broadcast TV stations are part of a national chain of stations called a network. The network provides programs for its member stations, or affiliates, to share. Local stations produce some of their own programs, but most of the day is filled with network programming, delivered to affiliates by satellite.

The three networks that have the most member stations in the United States are NBC, ABC, and CBS. In 1965, nearly all of the evening audience was watching network programming. By 1995, the networks' share of this audience had been cut almost in half. Cable television was one culprit, luring the audience away from the networks with many new viewing options.

A rating company estimates the number of people who are watching TV, and what shows they are watching.

Ratings experts can't call up everyone in the country to find out who's watching what. Instead, they keep an eye on the TV habits of sample viewers in each of over two hundred local television markets around the country.

Randomly chosen households in each area are sent TV diaries and viewers are asked to write down what they watch for a week.

I'll say I watched the ballet so they'll think I got class.

Diaries are mailed out during month-long ratings sweeps. Over 400,000 diaries a year are collected nationally.

Who's Watching? Who Cares?

Most broadcast TV stations and all cable systems in this country are commercial. They make money by selling broadcast time to businesses which want to promote their services or products. These advertisers want to reach the largest possible number of people with their message. So the more viewers a show has, the more money advertisers will pay to run commercials, or "ads," during that show. To find out how many people are watching TV programs, broadcasters and advertisers rely on a rating company.

A rating company also uses "people meters" to gather information about viewers. The meters are installed on TVs in a few thousand homes across the country, and are programmed with information about each member of the household.

Connected by phone lines to a central computer, the meters are used to estimate what the nation is watching each night.

The meter has a button for each person in the household to press every time he or she starts and stops watching TV.

AD RATES

More viewers mean higher advertising fees. Here are the costs for a thirty-second commercial today:

On a national network during the
  Super Bowl: **$1,000,000**
During prime time: **$100,000**
During a daytime soap opera: **$50,000**

On a local big-city station during a
  daytime soap: **$5,000**
During a late-night movie: **$600-$700**
During Sunday-morning kids' TV: **$300**

If used correctly, the meter records not only what shows are watched and when but also the age and sex of viewers.

Ratings based on people-meter data are computed at the end of the broadcast day and are delivered to broadcasters the following day.

PUBLIC TELEVISION

About 350 noncommercial TV stations in the United States are part of the Public Broadcasting System (PBS). They support themselves with grants from the government and from private foundations, and money donated by businesses and audience members.

Educational children's shows and programs on topics such as opera, painting, yoga, and woodworking do not attract a large number of viewers, so a commercial station would be unlikely to air them. But PBS is dedicated to bringing you just such programming.

Kids' TV Is Big Business

Seventy million children in the United States watch TV. A lot of TV. From ages two to eleven, they spend an average of three hours fourteen minutes a day in front of the set. Many businesses, from the makers of toys and breakfast cereals to fast-food restaurants and cookie companies, use TV to reach this audience.

What happened to penny candy?

DAD

Kids in the United States spend $9 billion of their own money a year, and influence their parents to spend another $14 billion.

To have an impact on how kids spend their money, advertisers try to dazzle them with ads. TV stations are allowed to sell between ten and a half and twelve minutes of advertising during every hour of children's programming.

In addition to creating effective ads, toy makers and other kid-oriented marketers have found that they can boost sales if their products are based on the characters in children's cartoons and action shows. Or, better yet, if the shows are based on toys they are already selling.

ELECTRIC ZAP

MUTANT KARATE RANGER SCOUTS® BODY ARMOR ($19.95)

M.K.R.S.® AM/FM RADIO HELM ($29.95)

M.K.R.S.® "LUNCH BOX OF POWER" ($12.95)

M.K.R.S® 1000 SQUIRT WATER BLASTER ($13.95)

M.K.R.S® SNEAKERS ($129.95)

M.K.R.S® KNEE PADS ($17.95)

Lucky I'm wearing my "Mutant Karate Ranger Scouts"® in-line skates!!!

However, it is against the law for commercials for these products to appear during the show they are connected with. Otherwise, the show and commercials together would become a continuous, thirty-minute advertisement for the products, instead of just exciting entertainment.

The large majority of toys sold in the United States are connected with TV shows or Hollywood movies. Producers of children's shows are constantly looking for new ideas for products to feature the characters in their shows, such as underwear, trading cards, snack foods, and soda glasses at fast-food chains.

On with the Show

Producing a children's variety show—or any TV show—involves careful step-by-step planning. Scripts have to be written for the host and the regular cast of characters. Special guests need to be found to provide something new and interesting for the regular characters to learn and talk about.

To plan a show, the producer, the director, and the host have a meeting.

The producer schedules the guests.

Then he writes the script, which is an outline of the show.

The script gets revised right up until air time.

On the day the show is to be taped, a production assistant keeps track of the guests as they arrive.

If someone can't go on, the staff has to think fast.

The director reviews the script and decides when guests come in and out of a scene.

She also goes over the script with the camera operators and the lighting crew.

During taping, she is in the control room, giving directions through a headset.

After the show is taped, a promotion director prepares a short advertisement, or "promo," for the show.

Shots of the whole scene are called wide-angle or overall shots.

The gaffer is the electrician responsible for proper lighting. Loaded with wires, stands, reflectors, and other equipment, the gaffer must figure out how to plug in the high-powered lights without blowing all the fuses.

The on-camera host has to be able to think fast on his feet and not lose control when startled, sick, or giggly. Hosts always check their hair and makeup, and are the best-paid members of the crew.

The sound engineer records the voices and sounds of what the camera sees. Wireless body mikes and their transmitters are hidden to keep them out of camera view. The sound person wears earphones to check sound levels, and to make sure that noises such as jet planes are not distracting.

The videographer is the "shooter," or camera person. A good shooter has the ability to catch a race-car spinout, a touchdown run, or an aerialist's somersault at the right instant, with one eye on the viewfinder and the other eye closed.

During a location shoot, the crew may videotape rehearsals and behind-the-scene action, interview performers, and then record the performance itself, to give a complete picture of the experience.

On Location

Performers such as lion tamers and trick riders cannot easily bring what they do into a TV studio. So a crew from a studio show sometimes goes to the circus, the rodeo, or other locations, to videotape events which will be edited into the program back at the station.

The director is the on-location boss who makes sure the crew shoots all the necessary video pieces that will be put together later. The director's biggest problems on location are people waving and making funny faces in the background, and, if the shoot is outside, rain.

How about a shot of this!

Get those clowns out of here!

DIRECTOR

GOFER

Sometimes called a gofer, a production assistant is usually someone just starting out in the business who "goes for" whatever the crew needs: coffee, lunch, or equipment from the van.

I'm only doing this ONCE!

Professional match-lighter (don't try this at home)

Here are the circus tapes and your pizza.

I hope I don't edit the pizza and eat the tape.

Tick Tick

Back at the station, a video editor will mix or arrange the location interviews, close-ups, and action shots, and add music and narration, according to the script.

Studio doors are big enough for a grand piano, an automobile, or a lion's cage to pass through.

(oof.)

Setting the Stage for Entertainment

Television can turn an empty studio with concrete floors and ceilings into a palace, a playground, a sailing ship, or a cozy living room. All it takes is a little scenery and a few good props.

The stage may look like a living room, but the studio looks like a barn, with hundreds of huge spotlights hanging from the beams. The flaps used to direct the light are called barn doors.

Programs that are produced five days a week, such as soap operas and talk shows, usually keep their sets and furnishings permanently in place. It would take too much time and money to reset and relight them every day.

The electricity used in three hours of lighting a TV show would light your house for a year.

The prop room is a giant closet with furniture, artificial trees, flowers, and the complete walls of room and building sets.

Who ordered a crate of real bananas?

Game shows can tape five episodes in one day, so the producers need to rent a soundstage for only a few weeks to create a whole year's worth of programs.

THE BIG SPIN OFF

Contestants have to compete just to get on the show. Producers pick those who are the most interesting and enthusiastic.

The hosts and contestants change clothes between sessions to make it look as if the shows were done on different days.

Studio floors are perfectly level, so the picture won't jiggle when cameras roll across the floor.

The set is taken apart and stored between tapings.

TV people wear makeup to cover their freckles and hide their wrinkles, so they look good under the bright studio lights. There are very few bald-headed men on TV—most wear toupees!

I hope I don't make a fool of myself.

Guests about to appear on a TV program wait in the green room. These waiting rooms were once thought to be more calming decorated in green, but are no longer painted just this color.

An opening wide shot is used to establish the setting for a scene.

Grips are responsible for setting up the equipment that holds the cameras.

In a rail shot, a camera mounted on a special dolly moves smoothly alongside the action.

The main crew does not waste time setting up and shooting simple detail shots. These are recorded later, by a smaller crew.

Rearview mirrors are sometimes removed on windshield shots.

In shots that don't feature the lead actor's face, a stand-in actor can be used.

Lights! Camera! Action!

Prime-time programs such as detective stories, dramas, and made-for-TV movies are complicated, expensive productions. It can take days to shoot just one scene that in the final program will last only a minute or two. This is because most scenes in the show are made up of film or video taken from many different camera positions, and the shot from each position is often recorded several times.

The action for each camera shot or cut is usually recorded more than once, until the director is satisfied he's gotten the effects he wants.

Was that good for you?

Background music and sound effects such as police sirens will be added in later.

DIRECTOR

more angst!

A reaction shot captures a character's response to a surprise.

For each cut, the actors retrace every step exactly the same as in previous cuts, so that the action will look identical from any angle when edited into a single scene.

stunt Double! let's go!

In dangerous scenes, stand-in stunt people are wigged and dressed to look like the actors.

TV dramas always break for commercials at exciting moments, so viewers will stay tuned.

The Television Prompter

When a soap star stares into her true love's eyes and pours out her innermost feelings, the words may seem to come straight from the heart—but actually she's just looking into the TV prompter and reading the script.

The words are moving too fast!

Oh, Doctor, I think I love you...

Scripts are typed into a computer and sent to a TV monitor mounted beneath the front of the camera.

The words on the monitor screen are reflected in a two-way mirror in front of the camera lens.

The two-way mirror is reflective only on the actress's side. The camera doesn't "see" the words from the other side, so they are invisible to the viewer.

Two-way mirror

Lens

Monitor

Script in reverse

The prompter operator can make the words move faster or slower, depending on how fast the actress reads.

Oh, Doctor, I think I... Hey!!

Is this my speech?

The President of the United States uses a TV prompter when he gives speeches. The text is reflected on glass panels in front of him.

She reads so slow I can't believe it!

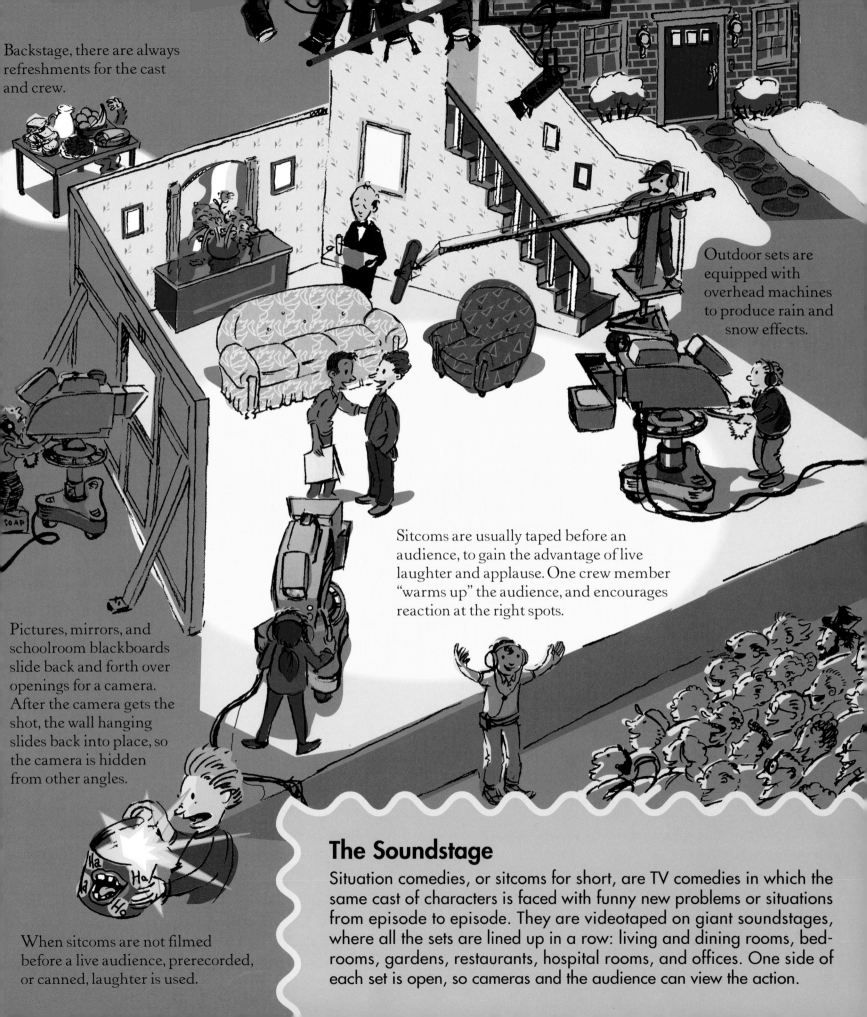

Backstage, there are always refreshments for the cast and crew.

Outdoor sets are equipped with overhead machines to produce rain and snow effects.

Pictures, mirrors, and schoolroom blackboards slide back and forth over openings for a camera. After the camera gets the shot, the wall hanging slides back into place, so the camera is hidden from other angles.

Sitcoms are usually taped before an audience, to gain the advantage of live laughter and applause. One crew member "warms up" the audience, and encourages reaction at the right spots.

When sitcoms are not filmed before a live audience, prerecorded, or canned, laughter is used.

The Soundstage

Situation comedies, or sitcoms for short, are TV comedies in which the same cast of characters is faced with funny new problems or situations from episode to episode. They are videotaped on giant soundstages, where all the sets are lined up in a row: living and dining rooms, bedrooms, gardens, restaurants, hospital rooms, and offices. One side of each set is open, so cameras and the audience can view the action.

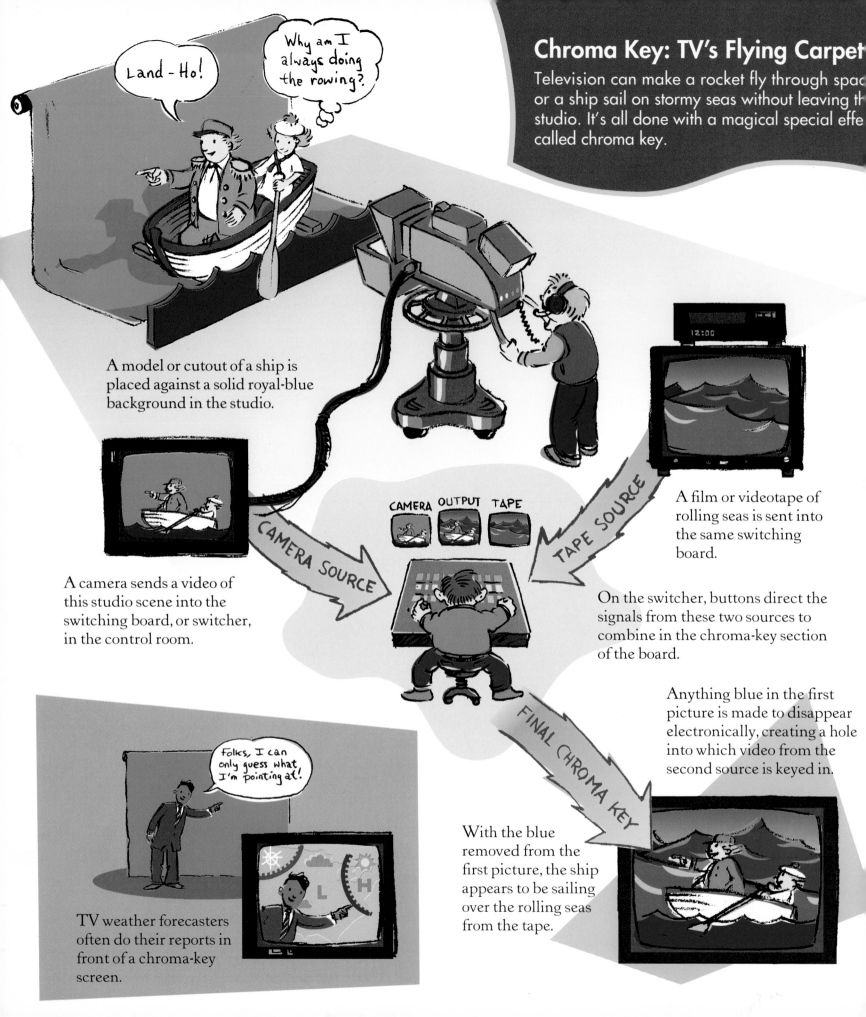

Chroma Key: TV's Flying Carpet

Television can make a rocket fly through space or a ship sail on stormy seas without leaving the studio. It's all done with a magical special effect called chroma key.

A model or cutout of a ship is placed against a solid royal-blue background in the studio.

A camera sends a video of this studio scene into the switching board, or switcher, in the control room.

CAMERA SOURCE

CAMERA   OUTPUT   TAPE

TAPE SOURCE

A film or videotape of rolling seas is sent into the same switching board.

On the switcher, buttons direct the signals from these two sources to combine in the chroma-key section of the board.

Anything blue in the first picture is made to disappear electronically, creating a hole into which video from the second source is keyed in.

FINAL CHROMA KEY

With the blue removed from the first picture, the ship appears to be sailing over the rolling seas from the tape.

TV weather forecasters often do their reports in front of a chroma-key screen.

Sign Language Spoken Here

People on TV can't glance up at a clock or down at a wrist-watch during a broadcast. It would look too awkward. So a floor manager keeps track of the time and gives this information to the on-air performer, using hand signals. He gives silent signals, or cues, so the TV viewers don't hear him.

Fingers count down the minutes remaining in a broadcast.

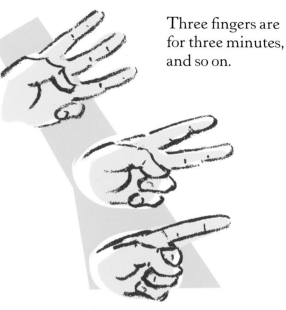

Three fingers are for three minutes, and so on.

A fist stands for fifteen seconds.

Crossed forefingers mean thirty seconds are left to go.

Fingers also count down the seconds. When there are only ten seconds to go, the floor manager counts down every second.

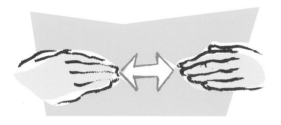

Hands pulling imaginary space apart mean "Stretch it out" or "Slow down."

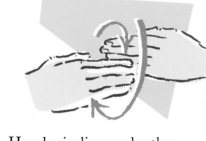

Hands circling each other mean "Speed up."

Pointing and making circles with the forefinger means "Finish up" or "Wrap it up."

Headphones to hear the director with. →

If I had a free hand I'd scratch my nose

GO TO COMMERCIAL BREAK

Battery and transmitter

old sneaks

During parades and variety shows, the floor manager will often send messages to the hosts using poster boards written on with wide felt-tip pens. These cue cards can suggest jokes and interview questions, or remind the host of the name of the next guest.

A slicing motion across the neck means "Cut" or "Stop now."

Choreographing Sports Coverage

Studio and news shows use two or three cameras. Sitcoms, soaps, and national talk shows might use four. But more than sixteen cameras and a crew of forty people are used to cover a professional football game for network television.

Miniature cameras are sometimes placed right inside players' helmets and referees' caps to take the viewer into the thick of the game.

Ten cameras are set up in fixed positions around the stadium.

A camera suspended from a blimp flying overhead will sometimes supply an aerial view.

Helmet-Cam ↗

Blimp-Cam ↘

IF WE SELL IT — THEN IT'S GOOD-NUF RAH!!!

The control truck, which has in it the director, sound and video engineers, and all the equipment found in a station control room, is parked outside the stadium.

The head referee is equipped with a wireless microphone so viewers can hear him announce penalties and decisions.

Game sounds are captured by special microphones that can be held on the sidelines and aimed at the field to pick up all the thuds of punts and all the grunts and groans of players.

From the nearby satellite uplink van, the game is sent to the network studios, then back out to a satellite, to be beamed to the local stations.

Ten-Yard PENALTY!

mama.

CBS ABC NBC FOX SHOE-TV

ASSIGNMENT EDITOR

A monkey has been spotted downtown!

The newsroom team plans the show, goes out on assignments, and puts the stories together.

PRODUCER

Send the news van! We'll do a live report!

Hey, leave some time for sports — I've got an exclusive interview with the new coach!

SPORTS EDITOR

REPORTER

All the boss says is: 'KEEP IT SHORT — your report can't run longer than two minutes.'

You'll lose all my best shots.

Too bad, buddy. Chop chop.

CAMERA OPERATOR

VIDEO EDITOR

Send the paddy wagon! We'll catch those monkeys

The Newsroom Is a Busy Place

It takes about forty people eight hours to put together one half-hour news show. Every day is like a relay race, with different teams racing to help each other make the finish line—show time.

Following cues from the director, the technical director determines what camera or tape is on the air, and can lay in graphics or video over the studio camera shots. He works the switcher, which has controls for each camera, videotape, and remote input, and for many special effects.

Who's the Boss?

There is a very strict chain of command in the control room. Without it, no one would know whose orders to follow. The producer decides how all the parts should fit together and finalizes the rundown for the director. But once they are in the control room, the director is the boss.

The director's job is a juggling act. He has to look at what is on the air—what the TV viewers at home are seeing—and at what is coming up next.

REMOTE 1

CAMERA 1

PREVIEW

REMOTE 2

CAMERA 2

ACTION NEWS 2 LIVE AT 5:00

EFFECT

ACTION NEWS 2 LIVE AT 5:00

TAPE

LIVE

Are we ready with the remote?

Get ready, camera one ... camera two, stand by for a close-up on Jeff...

Title tape is rolling.

I'll chroma-key the live shot over Jim's shoulder.

PRODUCER

TECHNICAL DIRECTOR

DIRECTOR

SOUND ENGINEER

VIDEOTAPE OPERATOR

Theme rolling.

The audio person sits at a control board with buttons and knobs to adjust every source of sound in the show. If you see someone talking but can't hear anything, it's usually because the audio person forgot to turn up the sound.

Stories sent in from reporters are put on videotape. About twenty-five of these tapes are used during a half-hour news show.

In the studio, the floor manager and camera people wear headsets so they can communicate with the director in the control room.

The camera operators adjust the focus and position of their cameras throughout the show, following instructions from the director.

The producer can talk to the anchors through special earpieces that look like hearing aids. He gives them up-to-the-minute information during the show.

A red indicator light on top of each camera lets the anchors know which one is on.

Jeff, we're going to lead with the monkey story.

Uh... my name is Jim.

CAMERA OPERATOR

CAMERA ①

ANCHORS

prompter

Two minutes to air.

rundown

During the show, the floor manager gives signals to the anchors.

FLOOR MANAGER

News anchors always seem dressed up when they are sitting behind the news desk, but they may not be from the waist down.

And this is what we see.

Only a monkey would wear that tie.

There's no monkeying around with tonight's big story about two escaped monkeys.

Our reporter, Monica, is live on the scene.

ACTION NEWS ②

The anchors sit in the studio and read the news, sports, and weather forecast. They're called anchors because they keep the show in place while delivering news from all over the world.

Microwaves Can Do More Than Cook Dinner

The TV news van is a mini television station on wheels. It can send local news stories back to the station as they are happening. This is called a remote shot. The pictures are being "shot" by the camera at a "remote" or distant place, sent back to the station as microwave signals, and broadcast directly to the TV viewers.

KFUN

KFUN VAN

mt. Kazoo

If a news van is more than thirty miles from a station, or is behind a hill, it uses relay towers to send the signal.

A microwave oven uses the same kind of power the news van uses to send its signal. When you heat a cup of water in the microwave oven, it absorbs the energy and weakens the microwaves.

In the same way, the microwave signal a news van sends out is weakened by moisture in tree leaves, or from rain or snow. This can make the picture on your TV screen look fuzzy.

An antenna on top of the news van is aimed at the station. It is on a telescoping pole that can be raised over forty feet. That's high enough to send a microwave signal to a station thirty miles away.

MICROWAVE OVEN

Hot dog

The news van is equipped so that a reporter may preview videotapes and write the script for a news story on the way back to the station, where the editing will be done.

KFUN
ACTION NEWS

The camera is connected to an antenna mounted underneath the helicopter that can be aimed at a microwave TV tower, to send the pictures directly to the station and out to the viewers.

Helicopters are a TV station's eyes in the sky. A cameraman or woman may go up in a helicopter to get a dramatic picture of a fire or a highway accident.

Program Cleared for Takeoff!

Engineers in the master control room are in complete control of all video and sound received, produced, and broadcast by a station. In many ways, master control is like an airport's control tower, except that at a television station there are many "runways" in, but only one main "runway" out—the broadcast channel.

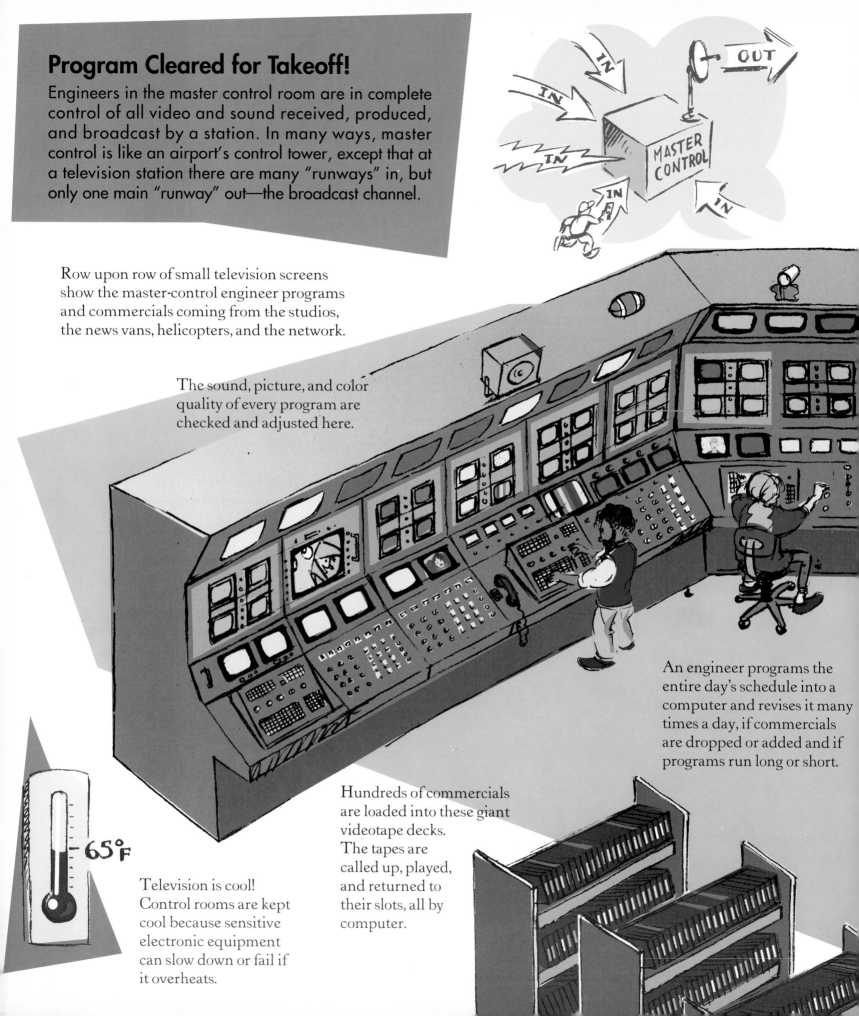

Row upon row of small television screens show the master-control engineer programs and commercials coming from the studios, the news vans, helicopters, and the network.

The sound, picture, and color quality of every program are checked and adjusted here.

An engineer programs the entire day's schedule into a computer and revises it many times a day, if commercials are dropped or added and if programs run long or short.

Hundreds of commercials are loaded into these giant videotape decks. The tapes are called up, played, and returned to their slots, all by computer.

—65°F

Television is cool! Control rooms are kept cool because sensitive electronic equipment can slow down or fail if it overheats.

All across the United States, TV stations set their clocks to match a master clock at radio station WWV in Fort Collins, Colorado. Television programs run exactly on time—to the second!

Nearly all the programming that a station receives from a network, other stations, and program producers is delivered by satellites.

Some of the same dishes that receive TV signals from satellites can also send local feeds out to the network and other stations.

Master control records all programs produced by the station. It also tapes incoming programs from the satellite dishes on the station lawn or roof.

If a big news story comes up and the station wants to cut into a program with a news bulletin, an engineer will override the computer schedule. He also takes over if there is a problem.

1927: Electronic, black-and-white TV system is unveiled.

1930: Broadcast of first TV drama.

1941: The first TV commercial airs—cost: $9.00.

1948: Primitive cable TV system created in Pennsylvania.

1951: First coast-to-coast telecast.

1953: Color TV system approved for use.

1956: Introduction of videotape recording.

1928: First home in United States gets a TV set.

1939: TV demonstrations at New York World's Fair draw huge crowds.

1946: Sales of TV sets boom after World War II, and stations begin broadcasting four or five nights a week.

1949: TV sets first appear in Sears catalogue.

1952: There are 52 million TV sets in the United States (pop. 152 million).

1954: Introduction of frozen TV dinners.

You will watch these pictures on screens that are measured in feet rather than inches, and are flat enough to hang on the wall.

Technicians are working to develop HDTV or high-definition television pictures that will look as clear as a scene viewed through a window.

With a telephone attached to the TV set, you'll be able to stay home sick and still be in your classes at school, taking notes and answering the teacher's questions.

You will make your own shows and "broadcast" them on a worldwide computer network for others to see.

Programming the Future

The television universe is always expanding. For its first half century, television talked and people watched. But now two-way television is becoming a reality, and people will soon be able to talk back. As home computers become more powerful and are linked to the television and phone lines, people will be able to do things they could never do before.

1962: Telstar I inaugurates satellite relays of TV programs.

1964: Instant replay increasingly used in sportscasts.

1967: Super Bowl I is broadcast.

1971: Color TV pictures of Apollo 14 moon landing are transmitted back to Earth.

1972: Launch of first national cable channel, Home Box Office (HBO).

1977: Tests of fiber-optic cable system in Chicago.

1987: People meters now in use in the United States.

1964: Over a thousand community antenna cable systems in operation.

1966: Networks airing nearly all their shows in color.

1969: 723 million viewers worldwide watch as man walks on the moon.

1971: Cigarette ads banned from TV.

1975: Home video-cassette recorders (VCRs) introduced.

1982: Boom in cable TV, with many new channels established.

1994: TV service from direct-broadcast satellites (DBS) inaugurated.

You will talk to your doctor on the phone while she displays your X-ray on the TV screen.

You will travel anywhere in the world by dialing up live video from exotic locations.

You will call a special movie-listing number to pick from any movie ever made.

You will be able to call up video images of any book in any library and turn the pages.

In the future, it is possible that our contacts with any life on other planets will be on television. That's because TV signals that shoot out from Earth travel on forever. If there are living creatures on some planet at the end of the galaxy, and if they have developed a TV technology similar to ours, they might be watching our television shows, just as we might someday be watching theirs.

For Abi and Ashley, my twin granddaughters
—W.C.M.

To Lindsay
—L.C.R.

For Norton
—M.C.

Thanks to Tom Bruemmer, Steve Capus, Dick Goggin, Alan Maslin,
Thomas Michener, Woody Reeves, Bob Ross, Joel Sanders, Donald Sharp, and Valari Staab.
Special thanks to broadcaster Lewis Klein.

Library of Congress Cataloging-in-Publication Data
Merbreier, W. Carter.
Television: what's behind what you see / W. Carter Merbreier
with Linda Capus Riley; pictures by Michael Chesworth.
p. cm.
1. Television – Juvenile literature. [1.Television.] I. Riley, Linda Capus. II. Chesworth, Michael, ill. III. Title.
TK6640.M47 1995 384.55 –dc20 95-13605 CIP AC